Something's Missing - the Fear of the Lord

Roger London

"Therefore let us be grateful for receiving a kingdom that cannot be shaken, and thus let us offer to God acceptable worship, with reverence and awe; for our God is a consuming fire."
(Hebrews 12:28-29)

Something's Missing - The Fear of the Lord

First published in Great Britain in 2014 by
Much Fruit Publishing
muchfruitpublishing@gmail.com

Copyright © 2014 Roger London

A catalogue record for this book is
available from the British Library

ISBN 978-0-9928955-1-8

Printed and bound in Uganda by
Mentart Design, Kampala

Cover design by **Roopop Design**

Something's Missing – the Fear of the Lord

Contents

Foreword

Sometimes, as Christian believers, we fail to come to an in-depth understanding of the need to live transformed lives. This can happen if we miss out on important revelation of some Biblical truth. Based on the fact that we are living in a generation which has not seen much of the mighty works and holy judgments of God, as did believers in the Old Testament and early Church days, many end up having a faith based solely on a loving God, one who is always full of mercy and grace. In fact, we can end up living in a way where we only see the merciful side of providence from our Heavenly Father.

As a Pastor, I have taken some time to consider the lifestyle of a number of believers who live their lives in a cycle of 'falling into sin and repenting', often indulging in the same sins they have repented of time and time again. The underlying assumption is that God will always overlook their iniquities, an assumption based on the fact that few have experienced anything of God's holy judgment as a reminder to them that the God of the Old Testament is still the same God today. Our forerunner and Elder John, in chapter two of his first letter, emphasizes that it is those who know Him who is from the beginning – the One who spans both the Old and New Testament days - who are considered to be mature in the faith. Their deep understanding of God's nature and His ways results in a consistent and transformed life.

I therefore count it a special privilege to write a foreword for this book because we all need to have a fuller understanding of God's Word and God's character. This book provides that which has been missing and more. It is a book one should read and own and even pass on to others.

Roger and his wife, Glenys, are good friends of mine – we have been working together in the ministry of Watchmen International for many years, both teaching and training church leaders and believers. They have a real passion and a genuine desire to see the wider Church prepared fully for the soon and second coming of Jesus Christ. You will sense this for yourself as you venture to read this book.

An important part of our calling as Christians is to develop a full understanding of Him who is from the beginning, who is now and who will always be – this revelation will lead us to daily live transformed lives, being changed from one degree of glory to another. I have no doubt, as you read through this book and apply it to your own life that you will never be the same again.

Stephen Nsibambi
(African International Coordinator for Watchmen International, Uganda)

Something's Missing - The Fear of the Lord

Introduction

Over the past fifty years the Holy Spirit has been restoring so much to the Church at large - teachings and experiences which had been largely lost throughout the centuries of Church history. These include an understanding and experience of the work of the Holy Spirit, especially His power and His gifts; an understanding of the Church as the Body of Christ expressed locally in committed relationships to one another; an understanding of the five-fold ministry giftings referred to in Ephesians chapter 4 - appreciating their fundamental significance in building church; a fresh experience of the wonder of praise and worship as we learn to live in the presence of God. The truth is we could add many more things to this list as we reflect on the extensive restoration work of the Holy Spirit in these last days before Jesus returns.

However, sometime back, I came to see that there is something which has been missing in the Church at large, something so fundamental, so vital. In fact, I would go so far as to say that without it, the Church cannot possibly be prepared as the Bride of Christ ready for the return of the Bridegroom. This missing factor is the fear of the Lord.

My personal confession is, that for many years, as a Pastor and church leader, I had never taught on the fear of the Lord - I had a vague understanding of what it was, but I had successfully circumnavigated the subject for over thirty years of Christian ministry. I guess that this would be the testimony

Something's Missing - The Fear of the Lord

of many pastors and leaders in the Church today. For all of us, the key to any spiritual breakthrough in understanding and experience is receiving revelation from the Holy Spirit – this would certainly have been the vehicle through which all the above teachings have been restored to the Church in recent decades. Paul's prayer for the Ephesian church in chapter one of his letter is that the Father of glory would give to them a spirit of wisdom and revelation in the knowledge of Him, having the eyes of their hearts enlightened (Ephesians 1:17-18). For me, with regard to the fear of the Lord, this prayer has certainly been answered.

In Proverbs we read:
"The fear of the Lord is the *beginning* of wisdom" (Proverbs 1:7)

This is repeated later in the same book:
"The fear of the Lord is the *beginning* of wisdom, and the knowledge of the Holy One is insight" (Proverbs 9:10)

My understanding of these verses is that there is something written here which is foundational, something which is critical to our understanding of God's nature and our response to Him. One of the things that I regularly pray for, having been in Christian ministry for many years, is wisdom. I have come to learn that wisdom is essential to everything else we might want to teach and experience in the Christian life. Solomon, who chose wisdom over riches and wealth, writes that the fear of the Lord is the very starting place in our acquiring of spiritual wisdom.

Something's Missing - The Fear of the Lord

I believe I had viewed the fear of the Lord as an Old Testament teaching, one which had been superseded by the era of God's grace. After all, how could we still fear the One who has been so clearly revealed to us as a loving Father? The fear of the Lord may be a tool which helps to bring a person to the Lord, but it quickly dissipates in the light of His grace and mercy. Doesn't the New Testament itself teach us that perfect love casts out all fear? However, as we shall see, this is clearly not what is meant. The fear of the Lord, which is birthed out of a revelation of God's holy nature is essential for us to truly appreciate the grace of God. I believe that the will of God is that we come to a place where we live out our Christian lives with the fear of the Lord and the grace of God beautifully intertwined.

Something's Missing - The Fear of the Lord

Something's Missing - The Fear of the Lord

Rediscovering the Holiness of God

It is clear from a study of both the Old and New Testaments that the fear of the Lord follows on from a revelation of the nature and character of God and an experience of His awesome acts.

We have become so used to concentrating on aspects of God's nature such as His grace, love, mercy, faithfulness, patience and His Fatherhood, that other aspects, equally as important, have been seriously overlooked – such as His holiness, righteousness, purity and awesomeness. This imbalance has been born out of a belief that the Old Testament reveals the holiness and judgment of God, whereas the New Testament, in unveiling the new covenant that God has made with His people, reveals His grace – often considered, at least unconsciously, as a quality which supersedes and cancels out all previous revelation. We also live in an age of spiritual sentiment where many Christians find it inconceivable that God still steps into history, even into the lives of individuals, in holy judgement. The majority of sermons and songs within our churches are seriously lacking in any mention of God's holiness and judgments. Believe it or not, the Old Testament is full of the grace and mercy of God; equally so, the New Testament often speaks of God's holiness and judgments. The last book of the Bible, so neglected in today's Church, is largely about God's coming judgment on an unbelieving world with the prospect of the lake of fire for all those who reject Jesus Christ as Lord and Saviour.

Something's Missing - The Fear of the Lord

I have come to the conclusion that the holiness of God is the chief aspect of God's nature. By holiness I mean that aspect of God's nature which is totally pure, completely separate from sin, can in no way, whatsoever, tolerate sin in any shape or form. My conclusion is based on the fact that there are only two references in the whole of the Bible where any aspect of God's nature is ever referred to in a tri-fold way and these references both refer to His holiness.

In Isaiah, chapter 6, we read of the prophet Isaiah's wonderful vision of God:
"In the year that King Uzziah died I saw the Lord sitting upon a throne, high and lifted up; and His train filled the temple. Above Him stood the seraphim; each had six wings: with two he covered his face, and with two he covered his feet, and with two he flew. And one called to another and said: '*Holy, holy, holy* is the Lord of hosts; the whole earth is full of His glory.' And the foundations of the threshold shook at the voice of him who called, and the house was filled with smoke." (Isaiah 6:1-4)

Note how the holiness of God is proclaimed three times by the seraphim. Note also how even they, as permanent residents of heaven, could not look directly at this awesome and holy God. Isaiah responds to this wonderful vision by declaring his utter ruin and sinfulness in the light of God's glory and holiness. There is no reason to suspect Isaiah to be a particularly sinful person; in fact, it is highly likely that he had a heart after God and was a faithful and obedient servant. However, when brought into the environment of God's absolute purity, he saw only his own sinfulness.

Something's Missing - The Fear of the Lord

It is interesting to note that just two chapters later in his prophecy, Isaiah states:
"Do not call conspiracy all that this people call conspiracy, and do not fear what they fear, nor be in dread. But the Lord of hosts, Him you shall regard as holy; let him be your fear, and let Him be your dread" (Isaiah 8:12-13)

Notice how Isaiah uses the same title – the Lord of hosts – to refer to God as was revealed to him in chapter 6. Isaiah's revelation of God's holiness clearly appears to have birthed in him an awesome fear of God.

In Revelation chapter 4, the apostle John wrote about a similar vision of God in His heavenly throne-room. Having described the glory and beauty of the throne-room and of the One who sat on the throne, John turns his attention to the creatures around the throne:
"And the four living creatures, each of them with six wings, are full of eyes all around and within, and day and night they never cease to sing, '*Holy, holy, holy*, is the Lord God Almighty, who was and is and is to come!'" (Revelation 4:8)

Amazingly, this tri-fold declaration of God's holiness is never-ending in heaven and throughout eternity! Note how the response of the twenty four elders to this ceaseless declaration of God's holiness was one of humble prostration, worship and song, declaring God's worth to receive glory, honour and power.

If the holiness of God is so clearly set apart in both the Old and New Testament by the declaration 'Holy, holy, holy', and

Something's Missing - The Fear of the Lord

if this is a never-ending proclamation in Heaven, resulting in eternal praise and adoration, then surely we need to pay much more attention to this both in our churches and also in our personal lives.

It is worth pointing out, that when you study revivals which have taken place in the Church throughout recent centuries, certain emphases are ever-present. These emphases include the revelation of God's holiness, resulting in the fear of the Lord, a deep conviction of sin leading to repentance and forgiveness. Doesn't this remind you of Isaiah, his heavenly vision and his repentant response to God?

The apostle Peter, in writing his first letter to believers, quotes from the Old Testament book of Leviticus. Clearly in Peter's mind God hadn't changed – the God who revealed Himself as holy under the old covenant was still the same holy God under the new covenant:
"As He who called you is holy, be holy yourselves in all your conduct; since it is written, 'You shall be holy, for I am holy'." (1 Peter 1:15-16; Leviticus 11:44)

In Revelation chapter 15 we have another glimpse into heaven, referring to all those who have triumphantly come through the final tribulation. John writes:
"And they sing the song of Moses, the servant of God, and the song of the Lamb, saying, "Great and wonderful are Thy deeds, O Lord God the Almighty! Just and true are Thy ways, O King of the ages! Who shall not fear and glorify Thy name, O Lord? For Thou alone art holy. All nations shall come and

worship Thee, for Thy judgments have been revealed"."
(Revelation 15:3-4)
This heavenly song is echoed in Psalm 89 where the Psalmist writes:
"Let the heavens praise Thy wonders, O Lord, Thy faithfulness in the assembly of the holy ones! For who in the skies can be compared to the Lord? Who among the heavenly beings is like the Lord, a God feared in the council of the holy ones, great and terrible above all that are round about Him." (verses 5-7)

Quite clearly, even at the end of this age, from those who come triumphantly through the final tribulation, there will still be an awesome fear of the One, who alone is holy, and whose name will continue to be 'Lord God Almighty' and 'King of the ages'.

In the great high-priestly prayer found in John chapter 17, Jesus, part way through his intercession, refers to His own Father as "Holy Father" (verse 13). This wasn't just a reverent reference to God by the earthly Jesus, not knowing His own identity as God's eternal Son. Rather this was a clear statement of the eternal nature and character of God by One who knew "that He had come from God and was going to God" (John 13:3). If Jesus reverences His Father as holy, then we certainly need to do the same. In fact, it is interesting that Jesus even couples together the holiness and fatherhood of God in the same breath. Much of our rejection of teaching on the holiness of God and the fear of the Lord comes out of what we would describe as a fresh revelation of God's Fatherhood, which we always couple together with His love and His fatherly care for His children. In this passage, Jesus clearly brings out the truth that any revelation of God's fatherhood must also and always embrace His holiness. This same coupling of the holiness and fatherhood of God is to be found at the beginning of the prayer that Jesus taught His disciples:

"Our Father who art in heaven, hallowed be Thy name" (Greek: 'hagiastheto' = hallowed, or separated, pure, revered as holy; Matthew 6:9).

In his first letter, Peter writes about a fatherhood which needs to be linked with the fear of a Holy Judge:

"And if you invoke as Father him who judges each one impartially according to his deeds, conduct yourself with fear (Greek: 'phobos' - see Chapter 2) throughout the time of your exile."

Much is attributed to the Holy Spirit in these days and His very name easily runs off our lips without any real consideration of who we are describing. In Romans chapter 1, Paul, at the beginning of his letter to the Roman believers, turns this name around and writes instead of "the Spirit of holiness" (verse 4). It would probably be a good practice in the Church today, if, for a season, we determined to always refer to the Spirit as the Spirit of holiness, until it was firmly fixed in our hearts and minds concerning the nature of the One who dwells within us.

There's No Escaping the Fact: Fear Really is Fear

In some translations of the New Testament, the word 'fear', when it is used in the context of the fear of the Lord, is translated as 'reverence' or 'respect'. There is clearly no justification for doing this and the practice appears to support the unwillingness or inability to couple together the grace of God with the holy fear of the Lord.

The New Testament Greek word, which is translated 'fear' (or reverence) in relation to the fear of the Lord is 'phobos' (noun) or 'phobeo' (verb). This is found in 2 Corinthians chapter 7:1, where the Corinthian believers are exhorted to "make holiness perfect in the *fear* (phobos) of God." This is the same common word used for translating 'fear', as in Matthew 14:26, when the disciples, battling the wind and the waves on a stormy Galilee night, "cried out for *fear*" (phobos) when they saw Jesus walking towards them on the water. It is also the same word used for the response of the crowd, having seen Jesus drive out the 'legion' of demons into the herd of pigs in the region of the Gerasenes. In Luke 8:37 it is stated that the local residents of that area "were seized with great *fear*" (phobos).

There are passages in the New Testament, where we might want to use the word 'reverence' or 'respect' in relation to the word 'phobos' For example, in Romans chapter 13, Paul speaks about respecting ruling authorities: he exhorts the believers to give "*respect* (phobos) to whom *respect* is due"

17

Something's Missing - The Fear of the Lord

(verse 7). However, the fact that the same Greek word is used, which is commonly translated as 'fear', clearly shows that the reverence and respect called for carried with it an understanding of the consequences if such respect is not given! Failure to pay taxes, for example, to the Roman Emperor, would carry the penalty of beatings, imprisonment and possible death! So there would have been a fear of disobeying the authorities.

Vines Expository Dictionary of New Testament Words states that the Greek word 'phobos' first had the meaning of *'flight'*, an intense desire to flee caused by being scared. It then came to mean *'fear'*, *'dread'* or *'terror'* In fact it is always used in this sense in the four gospels. In relation to the fear of the Lord, 'phobos' is described as a *wholesome dread of displeasing God*.

The Bible commentator and scholar, Hendricksen, says that the fear of the Lord is "being afraid to offend God in any way".

In Luke 12:4-5, Jesus uses the same Greek verb 'phobeo' to describe both the fear of men and the fear of God:
"I tell you, my friends, do not *fear* those who kill the body, and after that have no more that they can do. But I will warn you whom to *fear*: *fear* Him who, after He has killed, has power to cast into hell; yes, I tell you, *fear* Him!"

In Philippians 2:13, Paul exhorts the believers: "work out your salvation with *fear* (phobos) and *trembling*" (Greek: tromos = *trembling with fear, quaking, reverential awe*).

Something's Missing - The Fear of the Lord

In the Old Testament, the main Hebrew words which are used to translate 'fear', as in the fear of the Lord, are:
'Yare':
"Who considers the power of Thy anger, and Thy wrath according to the *fear* of Thee?" (Psalms 90:11)
O *fear* the Lord, you His saints, for those who *fear* Him have no want!" (Psalms 34:9)
and **'Yirah'**:
"The *fear* of the Lord is hatred of evil" (Proverbs 8:13)
"The *fear* of the Lord is the beginning of wisdom, and the knowledge of the Holy One is insight" (Proverbs 9:10).

These words literally mean '*fear*' or '*terror*'; they can also mean '*an awesome or terrifying thing*' and '*fear mingled with reverence or respect*'.

You may well be thinking at this point that it is fine to quote the scriptures used in this chapter but what about 1 John 4:18 where the Apostle John clearly states:
"There is no fear in love, but perfect love casts out fear. For fear has to do with punishment, and he who fears is not perfected in love." Surely this scripture puts all the above comments on the fear of the Lord to bed once and for all - the grace of God has done away with the fear of the Lord? In order to answer this, we need to remember two important guides to interpreting scripture: there is the guide of always interpreting a scripture from within its immediate context, and, secondly, all scripture needs to be interpreted within the context of the wider body of Scripture, namely, the whole of God's Word. To look at the immediate context then:

Something's Missing - The Fear of the Lord

in 1 John 4:17, John is speaking about the confidence true believers can have on the Day of Judgment. Therefore, in verse 18, he is specifically stating that there is no fear of the punishment of God's final judgment for all who abide in Christ and who abide in love. In this passage he has nothing to say about the fear of the Lord. Secondly, within the context of the wider body of Scripture – we find that there are countless scriptures referring to the fear of the Lord, covering both the Old and New Testaments, which includes those that refers to Jesus' own fear of God and others that stretch forward even into the eternal throne-room of God.

In Psalm 34, the Psalmist writes:
"I sought the Lord, and He answered me, and delivered me from all my fears" (verse 4).
However, within the next few verses, the Psalmist includes four references to fearing the Lord:
"O *fear the Lord*, you His saints, for *those who fear Him have no want!*" (verse 9; see also verses 7 and 11)

Certainly the Lord wants us to be free from all human-induced fears, including the fear of man, the fear of circumstances, the fear of sickness and death, and the fear of the future. However, the fear of the Lord is our ongoing response towards the awesome, majestic, and holy King of glory.

In concluding this chapter, let's hear the words of author and speaker, the late Mike Yaconelli:

Something's Missing - The Fear of the Lord

"We aren't afraid of God, we aren't afraid of Jesus, we aren't afraid of the Holy Spirit. As a result, we have ended up with a need-centred gospel that attracts thousands... but transforms no one. The mystics always talk about terror and I've never understood it, although I do now. It's the recognition of what truth means. Truth is frightening, terrifying. I'm not sure I really want to be with the truth which is why we work so hard to control it, suppress it, and take the life out of it. When the guys were in the boat when Jesus calmed the storm, I'm convinced that they were more afraid when the storm was over. They knew the terror of near death in a storm, but now they knew a new terror. The terror of a God who can calm a storm. And I don't think there are enough terrified people in the church. The church is made up of people who have God all figured out."

Something's Missing - The Fear of the Lord

Rediscovering the Grace of God

Today the grace of God appears to be the all-encompassing message of the wider Church. Make no mistake, firstly hearing about and then experiencing the grace of God is truly wonderful. Without the grace of God, all of us would be utterly lost and without hope in this world. All preachers and teachers of God's Word need to constantly come back to the theme of the grace of God. However, I have come to the position that none of us can have a full and proper understanding of God's grace, without firstly having a revelation of the utter holiness of God, a holiness which then produces within us the fear of the Lord.

Listen to what A. W. Tozer has to say on this subject:
"A truth fully taught in the Scriptures and verified in personal experience by countless numbers of holy men and women through the centuries might be condensed thus into a religious axiom: *No one can know the true grace of God who has not first known the fear of God*....Until we have been gripped by that nameless terror which results when an unholy creature is suddenly confronted by that One who is the holiest of all, we are not likely to be much affected by the doctrine of love and grace as it is declared by the New Testament evangel. The love of God affects a carnal heart not at all; or if at all, then adversely, for the knowledge that God loves us may simply confirm us in our self-righteousness. The effort of liberal and borderline modernists to woo men to God by presenting the soft side of religion is an unqualified evil because it ignores the very reason for our alienation from

Something's Missing - The Fear of the Lord

God in the first place. Until a man has gotten into trouble with his heart he is not likely to get out of trouble with God."

In Isaiah chapter 6, we read of Isaiah's encounter with the holiness of God, which clearly produced within him a wholesome dread of the Lord of hosts (Isaiah 8:13). Isaiah's first response to this incredible vision of the Lord was:
"Woe is me! For I am lost; I am a man of unclean lips, and I dwell in the midst of a people of unclean lips; for my eyes have seen the King, the Lord of hosts!"
In the light of God's utter holiness, Isaiah saw only his utter sinfulness. It was precisely at that point of revelation and remorse that the wonderful grace of God was extended to him:
"Then flew one of the seraphim to me, having in his hand a burning coal which he had taken with tongs from the altar. And he touched my mouth, and said, "Behold, this has touched your lips; your guilt is taken away, and your sin forgiven"." (verses 6-7)
Isaiah's experience of the gracious forgiveness of God was all the richer following his deathly assessment of himself, seeing himself as he truly was - heaped in sin - in the light of God's purity and holiness. Through this revelation, Isaiah knew his just deserts, but, instead, experienced the unexpected and unmerited forgiveness of the Lord of hosts!

Similarly in the New Testament, we read of the Apostle Paul's amazing encounter with the holiness of God on the road to Damascus Acts 9:1-19 and 22:6-16). Up until that point Paul would have seen himself as a defender of the righteousness of God, an upholder of God's holy law.

Something's Missing – The Fear of the Lord

However, there on that lonely road, Paul was struck down by the dazzling brilliance of God's holy presence, which he describes as "a great light from heaven" (Acts 22:6). There is no doubt in my mind that any fear of God Paul might previously have had would have been totally transformed into a living fear of a holy Lord Jesus. This must have been the occasion that gave birth to Paul's accurate assessment of himself in his first letter to Timothy, where he writes:

"The saying is sure and worthy of full acceptance, that Christ Jesus came into the world to save sinners. And I am the foremost of sinners; but I received mercy for this reason, that in me, as the foremost, Jesus Christ might display His perfect patience for an example to those who were to believe in him for eternal life" (1 Timothy 1:15-16).

We do a great injustice to Paul's profound teaching on the grace of God, as found in all of his letters, if we ignore the revelation of God's utter holiness that gave rise to the insight of Paul's depravity, which, in itself, gave God the wonderful opportunity to pour out His grace on this chief of sinners.

I am convinced that many today are 'born' into God's kingdom on the basis of New Testament teaching on the love and grace of God, but devoid of any encounter with His holiness leading to a deep conviction of sin and repentance. I am equally convinced that seeking to enter God's kingdom on the basis of hearing that God loves you accompanied by a simple prayer of 'accepting Jesus' is the single most factor leading to problems of spiritual growth in the lives of new believers.

Something's Missing - The Fear of the Lord

Each one of us needs to understand afresh that all we ever deserved from God was judgement and total separation from Him (what the Bible describes as hell) because of our sinfulness. For everyone who truly enters the kingdom of God, it has cost God everything – for the only way that He could possibly welcome us into His holy presence was to pour out his holy anger and judgment on His very own Son, Jesus. The true pain and agony of the cross was not the cruel physical and mental suffering which Jesus had to endure, but the overwhelming crushing impact of God's holy judgment poured into Jesus' mortal body as he hung there on the cross. The sweat drops of blood pouring from His brow in the garden of Gethsemane were in full anticipation of knowing the fearfulness of falling "into the hands of the Living God" (Hebrews 10:31). We were the ones who deserved this wrath and judgment – yes, even the 'not-so-bad' sinners as some might describe themselves. In the light of God's utter holiness, we would cry, as did Isaiah, bemoaning our gross uncleanness, hiding our faces in total shame from the brilliance of God's glory. Thanks be to God - Jesus took our place – such love, such grace! Hallelujah and hallelujah!

The Fear of the Lord in the Old Testament

As already stated at the beginning of Chapter 1, it is clear from a study of both the Old and New Testaments that the fear of the Lord follows on from a revelation of the nature and character of God and an experience of His awesome acts.

One of the earliest references to the fear of the Lord in the Old Testament is found in Genesis chapter 22. Here, Abraham, in obedience to the Lord, built an altar. He then bound and laid his son, Isaac, upon the wood and was about to slay him with a knife when the Lord spoke to him:
"Do not lay your hand on the lad or do anything to him; *for now I know that you fear God*, seeing that you have not withheld your son, your only son, from me." (Genesis 22:12)

Such was Abraham's fear of the Lord that disobedience was out of the question. Abraham had experienced enough of God's holy presence and power, and undoubtedly had heard much of His awesome acts which had led up to the point where he was even willing to sacrifice his only son if that was what God was asking of him.

Let's examine some of the Godly interventions which would have impacted upon Abraham and instilled within him a holy fear of the Lord: He would certainly have heard much of the judgment of God through a worldwide flood (Genesis 6:9 to 9:19) killing all of mankind apart from Noah and his family (Noah was still alive when Abraham was born). We know this story so well as a wonderful Sunday school story that the horror of mankind being totally destroyed in a devastating

27

flood is lost to us. We miss the screams and shrieks of drowning people as God used fearsome flood waters to judge wicked mankind. I am sure that Abraham would have been aware of this awesome act of God in all its detail as it was passed down from generation to generation. Abraham would have heard of the amazing God-induced confusion brought upon the people at the tower of Babel (Genesis 11:1-9), scattering them to the four corners of the earth. Again we miss the terrible fear which would have struck the hearts of the people as their ability to communicate with one another was removed in an instant as a result of God's judgment on their arrogance and pride. Abraham personally experienced God appearing before him as He promised great blessing on his future descendents. This included the time when "a deep sleep fell on Abram; and lo, a dread and great darkness fell upon him." On this occasion God passed before Abraham like a "smoking fire pot and a flaming torch" as a new covenant was forged between them (Genesis 15:12-20). I have no doubt that this dreadful and dark sleep, as God's awesome presence descended on Abraham, would have created yet a deeper understanding of the fear of the Lord within him. Abraham was around when God rained down his judgment on Sodom and Gomorrah with "brimstone and fire." He stood and observed smoke arising from those godless cities "like the smoke of a furnace" (Genesis 19:24-29). He would have had to handle the deep grief of his own nephew as Lot's wife was judged in an instant for looking back (and probably hankering after) her former home. Little wonder in the light of these, and other, incidences in Abraham's life, that he greatly feared God; little wonder that he was prepared to sacrifice his dearly loved son rather than disobey the One who had

Something's Missing - The Fear of the Lord

revealed Himself as El Shaddai - the Lord God Almighty! (Genesis 17:1)

Moses is another wonderful example as we further look at the fear of the Lord in the Old Testament. We begin with Moses' encounter with God in the wilderness. Here Moses, who had been a shepherd for many years, tending the flock of his father in law, Jethro, suddenly saw a very strange sight - a desert bush which was burning. A burning bush, in itself, would not have been an unusual occurrence - the unusual thing was that this flaming bush was not being consumed by the fire. As Moses approached, the Lord spoke to him from out of the bush. He warned Moses:

"Do not come near, put off your shoes from your feet, for the place on which are standing is holy ground ... I am the God of your father, the God of Abraham, the God of Isaac, and the God of Jacob."
(Exodus 3:6)

Moses' response was that he "hid his face, *for he was afraid to look at God*." Before him was none other than the Lord God Himself. This was the beginning of Moses' first-hand understanding of the holiness of God and the fear of the Lord.

Very soon after this encounter, when Moses had exhausted almost every avenue in trying to squirm out of obeying God's call on his life, we read of an incident which is often missed in relaying the story of the exodus of God's people from Egypt. In Exodus chapter 4:24 we read:

"At a lodging place on the way the Lord met him (i.e. Moses) and sought to kill him."

Something's Missing - The Fear of the Lord

We cannot glean from the context the exact reason as to why the Lord was going to judge Moses - was it Moses' reluctance and unwillingness to obey God's call on his life, or was it Moses' casual neglect of circumcising his own son? Whatever the reason, Moses was only saved through the quick thinking of his wife, Zipporah, who immediately circumcised their son and touched Moses' feet with it - a wonderful picture of blood (looking forward to Calvary) turning away God's wrath. Surely this event would have had a deep impact on Moses as he came within seconds of losing his life as a result of God's judgment on him! (verses 25-26)

Following this near miss on his own life, Moses then experienced the full extent of God's wrath poured out upon a nation, as plague after plague was sent by Him upon the Egyptians who had been mistreating the Israelite people (Exodus chapters 5-12). The end result was that even the first-born sons of all the Egyptians were killed in one night, an event which would have been horrific to hear and to observe - everywhere you looked there would have been families wailing at the sudden, unexpected deaths of their loved ones. Let's strip these accounts of any cartoon image of frogs and gnats and see them for what they were - accounts of a holy God intervening in righteous judgment in the lives of disobedient men, women and children.

Soon after this the Israelites were allowed to leave Egypt, but very quickly they encountered the impenetrable barrier of the Red Sea, as they were being hotly pursued by Pharaoh's army. Again, God acted in awesome judgment - no sooner had the Israelites crossed through the miraculously-opened

Something's Missing – The Fear of the Lord

waters when God completely enveloped the pursuing army with a fearful watery judgment. The true picture here would have been one of hundreds of dead and decaying bodies being washed up on the eastern shoreline before a shocked and fearful Israelite nation. The response of the people is recorded at the end of Exodus chapter 14:

"And Israel saw the great work which the Lord did against the Egyptians, and *the people feared the Lord* ..." (verse 31)

In Exodus chapter 15 we have an account of a song composed by the Israelites following this incredible event. It includes the following:

"Thy right hand, O Lord, glorious in power, Thy right hand, O Lord, shatters the enemy. In the greatness of Thy majesty Thou overthrowest Thy adversaries; Thou sendest forth Thy fury, it consumes them like stubble." (verses 6 and 7)

and:

"Who is like Thee, O Lord, among the gods? Who is like Thee, majestic in holiness, *terrible in glorious deeds*, doing wonders?" (verse 11 and 12)

In some translations we find the phrase *"awesome (or fearful) in splendour."* Such fear and awe of a holy God was invoked in all who experienced this act of judgment and deliverance, including Moses himself.

The last account we will look at in the life of Moses (although there are several more) was when Moses met with the Lord on Mount Sinai. The scene was one of a mountain cloaked in thick cloud, smoking like a kiln, shuddering as in an earthquake, surrounded with thunderings and lightning. The people had been strongly warned not to seek to climb or approach the edge of the mountain otherwise they would be put to death (Exodus 19:10-25). In the next chapter we read the following:

"Now when all the people perceived the thunderings and the lightnings and the sound of the trumpet and the mountain smoking, the people were afraid and trembled; and they stood afar off, and said to Moses, "You speak to us, and we will hear; but let not God speak to us, lest we die." And Moses said to the people, "Do not fear; for God has come to prove you, and that *the fear of Him may be before your eyes, that you may not sin*"." (Exodus 20:18-20)

Moses recounted this incident in Deuteronomy where he wrote:

"How on the day that you stood before the Lord your God at Horeb, the Lord said to me, 'Gather the people to me, that I may let them hear My words, so that *they may learn to fear me all the days that they live upon the earth*, and that they may teach their children so'." (Deuteronomy 4:10)

These real life incidents in the lives of Abraham, Moses and the children of Israel would have been faithfully and graphically passed down from one generation to another throughout Old Testament history. A clear understanding of God's holiness, His righteous judgments, His awesome majesty - all resulting in a holy fear of the Lord - would have been etched into the hearts and minds of God's covenant people. Time and time again, they disobeyed the Lord; time and time again, they were subject to His holy judgment on their sin. Each cycle of rebellion would simply have reinforced this understanding of God's holiness, His inability to overlook their sin, and the need to live their lives in the fear of Him.

The Fear of the Lord in the New Testament

Before looking into the fear of the Lord in the New testament, we need to understand the backdrop which the Old Testament provides on this subject We can only define the New Testament usage of the phrase 'the fear of the Lord' in the light of its unwrapping in the lives of people such as Abraham, Moses and the children of Israel. God does not change one iota when you step from the last verse of Malachi's prophecy into the first verse of Matthew's gospel – He is still the same holy, righteous, and awesome God.

A starting place for looking into the fear of the Lord in the New Testament is the person of Jesus Himself. Whilst the scripture below is from the Old Testament prophecy of Isaiah, it is a direct reference to the coming Messiah:
"And the Spirit of the Lord shall rest upon Him, the spirit of wisdom and understanding, the spirit of counsel and might, the spirit of knowledge and the *fear of the Lord*. And His delight shall be in the *fear of the Lord*." (Isaiah 11:2-3a)

This scripture is supported in the New Testament in the epistle to the Hebrews:
"In the days of His flesh, Jesus offered up prayers and supplications, with loud cries and tears, to Him who was able to save Him from death, and He was heard for His *godly fear*" (Greek: eulabeia = reverence, holy fear. Hebrews 5:7).

Jesus, God's bridge between the Old and the New Covenants, delighted in the fear of the Lord. Even for Jesus, in His life on earth, to have a spirit of wisdom and understanding it was

35

necessary for Him to understand and live in the fear of the Lord.

We have seen already, in Luke 12, how Jesus exhorted his listeners to fear God:

"I tell you, my friends, do not fear those who kill the body, and after that have no more that they can do. But I will warn you whom to *fear*: *fear* Him who, after He has killed, has power to cast into hell; yes, I tell you, *fear* Him!" (verses 4-5)

The Acts of the Apostles is where we discover so much about New Testament church life. In the first few chapters we find out about the vibrancy of the power of the Holy Spirit upon those first disciples; we see the centrality of waiting on God in prayer; we observe the total and practical commitment that the disciples had for one another. We also see a very clear example of how the Holy Spirit ensured that the fear of the Lord was instilled into those new believers.

In Acts chapter 5 we have an account of a couple named Ananias and Sapphira. The context would indicate that these were amongst the group that would call themselves disciples of Jesus. Many in that new Jerusalem church, moved by the Spirit, had sold houses and lands in order to release money for those in need. Ananias and Sapphira also sold some property but they had decided to keep back a large part of the money for themselves. In itself there was nothing wrong in such action, but, again, the context would indicate that they were intending their generous gift to be seen by those in the church as a total offering, a sacrificial gift – they intended to deceive. As soon as Ananias laid the gift at the

Something's Missing – The Fear of the Lord

Apostles' feet, Peter challenged him with a soul-piercing question:

"Ananias, why has Satan filled your heart to lie to the Holy Spirit and to keep back part of the proceeds of the land? While it remained unsold, did it not remain your own? And after it was sold, was it not at your disposal? How is it that you have contrived this deed in your heart? You have not lied to men but to God." (verses 3-4)

The result of this revealing challenge was that Ananias immediately fell down dead in the presence of everyone! Three hours later, Sapphira, his wife, was similarly challenged with the same end result. How did this awesome judgment of God affect those early believers? Verse 11 clearly states:

"And *great fear* (phobos) came upon the whole church, and upon all who heard of these things."

In verse 13, Luke adds in his account:

"None of the rest *dared* join them, but the people held them in high honour."

How could a loving and merciful God act in such a way to those who were testifying to be His children, especially so soon after the saving death of His own Son? Wouldn't this have been a supreme example of God's longsuffering to preserve their lives, especially as nobody had really been hurt by this small act of deception? Nobody would ever have known! The answer was – God knew! In His master plan to reach the world through this brand-new church, it was essential that they began as they needed to continue - to walk in the fear of the Lord. They needed to recognise that God's mighty presence amongst them was indeed nothing other than the presence of the One who has always been, and will always be reverenced as 'holy, holy, holy'.

Why doesn't God always act in this way? Perhaps many natural disasters, sicknesses and premature deaths today are, in fact, judgments of God, but there's no easy answer to such a question. One thing we know for sure though is that He can never overlook sin, in any shape or form, whether it affects any other person or not. There will be a day of reckoning for all unrepented sin in the lives of believers as well as unbelievers.

Sometimes, in times of spiritual revival in the Church, such cases, as that of Ananias and Sapphira, have come to light, as God's Holy presence powerfully breaks in amongst His people. I personally believe that we are rapidly approaching such a day again – it will be part of God's master plan in preparing a pure and spotless Bride for the return of His Son, Jesus – when we will find it impossible to seek to come into God's presence without clean hands and a pure heart (Psalms 24:3-4), without risking His immediate judgment on our sin. How can we prepare for such a time? Let's rediscover the holiness of God and the fear of the Lord. Proverbs 16 states: "By the fear of the Lord a man avoids evil." (verse 6)

In writing his first letter to a church beset with problems, Paul boldly states that the reason why many members of the church in Corinth were weak and ill, and some had even died, was due to their failure to discern the body of Christ. Paul states that they were guilt of "profaning (i.e. sinning against) the body and blood of the Lord" (1 Corinthians 11:27-32). Their sins against one another, their factions, jealousy and

Something's Missing - The Fear of the Lord

immorality were primarily offences against a Holy and Righteous God, who would not just sit back and allow these things to continue.

Returning to Acts, there is a very revealing verse:
"So the church throughout all Judea and Galilee and Samaria has peace and was built up; and walking in the *fear of the Lord* and in the comfort of the Holy Spirit it was multiplied." (Acts 9:31).
How many of us, when asked if we desire to see the Church, our church, built up and even multiplied, would cry out 'Yes, Lord'? Of course we would. Well this verse probably contains a powerful key in this process – yes, we will always need the encouraging work of the Holy Spirit, being able to move in His power and His gifts, but there is also a pressing need to walk, and keep on walking, in the fear of the Lord.
Let's look at some other New Testament scriptures which refer to the fear of the Lord:

"Be subject to one another out of *reverence for Christ* (literally in the fear – phobos – of God)." (Ephesians 5:21)

"Since we have these promises, beloved, let us cleanse ourselves from every defilement of body and spirit, and make holiness perfect in the *fear of God*." (2 Corinthians 7:1)

"Slaves, obey in everything those who are your earthly masters, not with eye-service, as men-pleasers, but in singleness of heart, *fearing the Lord*." (Colossians 3:22)

Something's Missing – The Fear of the Lord

"Therefore let us be grateful for receiving a kingdom that cannot be shaken, and thus let us offer to God acceptable worship, with reverence and *awe* (Greek: eulabeia); for our God is a consuming fire." (Hebrews 12:28-29)

"Honour all men. Love the brotherhood. *Fear God*. Honour the emperor." (1 Peter 2:17)

"And the twenty four elders who sit on their thrones before God fell on their faces and worshipped God, saying, "We give thanks to Thee, Lord God Almighty, who art and who wast, that Thou hast taken Thy great power and begun to reign. The nations raged, but Thy wrath came, and the time for the dead to be judged, for rewarding Thy servants, the prophets and saints, and those who *fear Thy name*, both small and great, and for destroying the destroyers of the earth"." (Revelation 11:16-18)

"The I saw another angel flying in mid-heaven, with an eternal gospel to proclaim to those who dwell on earth, to every nation and tribe and tongue and people; and he said with a loud voice, "*Fear God* and give Him glory, for the hour of His judgment has come; and worship Him who made heaven and earth, the sea and the fountains of water"." (Revelation 14:6-7)

"And they sing the song of Moses, the servant of God, and the song of the Lamb, saying, "Great and wonderful are Thy deeds, O Lord God the Almighty! Just and true are Thy ways, O King of the ages! Who shall not *fear and glorify Thy name*, O Lord? For Thou alone art holy. All nations shall come

Something's Missing – The Fear of the Lord

and worship Thee, for Thy judgments have been revealed"."
(Revelation 15:3-4)

These scriptures clearly illustrate that every aspect of our lives – our submission to one another, our walk of holiness, our daily employment, our worship - all need to be under-girded with the fear of the Lord. In fact, only a true understanding of God's holy nature, resulting in a fear of the Lord, is able to order our lives in the way God intended. The scriptures in Revelation appear to indicate that the fear of the Lord will never cease - even those who have triumphed through the final tribulation, when clothed in their royal garments as eternal sons, will still refer to God as Holy Father and fear His Holy Name!

Something's Missing - The Fear of the Lord

The Fear of the Lord: What could be better?

In this chapter I simply want to highlight a number of scriptures from the Psalms and Proverbs which speak of the benefits and blessings of fearing the Lord. In Africa, when teaching on this subject, I would normally begin by asking the question, "How many of you want to have a regular provision of food, enjoy long life, know healing and have the desires of your hearts fulfilled?" Of course the answer is "everyone" - well, take time to meditate on the scriptures that follow:

"But I through the abundance of Thy steadfast love will enter Thy house; I will worship toward Thy holy temple in the fear of Thee." (Psalm 5:7)

"The friendship of the Lord is for those who fear Him, and He makes known to them His covenant." (Psalm 25:14)

"O how abundant is Thy goodness, which Thou hast laid up for those who fear Thee." (Psalm 31:19)

"Behold, the eye of the Lord is on those who fear Him, on those who hope in His steadfast love, that He may deliver their soul from death, and keep them alive in famine." (Psalm 33:18-19)

"The angel of the Lord encamps around who fear Him, and delivers them." (Psalm 34:7)

"O fear the Lord, you His saints, for those who fear Him have no want!" (Psalm 34:9)

43

Something's Missing - The Fear of the Lord

"Thou hast set up a banner for those who fear Thee, to rally to it from the bow, that Thy beloved may be delivered." (Psalm 60:4-5)

"Surely his salvation is at hand for those who fear Him, that glory may dwell in our land." (Psalm 85:9)

"Teach me Thy way, O Lord, that I may walk in Thy truth; unite my heart to fear Thy name." (Psalm 86:11)

"For as the heavens are high above the earth, so great is His steadfast love toward those who fear Him." (Psalm 103:11)

"As a father pities his children, so the Lord pities those who fear Him." (Psalm 103:13)

"But the steadfast love of the Lord is from everlasting to everlasting upon those who fear Him." (Psalm 103:17)

"He provides food for those who fear Him; He is ever mindful of His covenant." (Psalm 111.5)

"The fear of the Lord is the beginning of wisdom; a good understanding have all those who practise it." (Psalm 111:10)

"You who fear the Lord, trust in the Lord! He is their help and their shield." (Psalm 115:11)

"He will bless those who fear the Lord, both small and great." (Psalm 115:13)

Something's Missing - The Fear of the Lord

"Confirm to Thy servant Thy promise, which is for those who fear Thee." (Psalm 119:38)

"He fulfils the desire of all who fear Him, He also hears their cry, and saves them." (Psalm 145:19)

"But the Lord takes pleasure in those who fear Him, in those who hope in His steadfast love." (Psalm 147:11)

"Be not wise in your own eyes; fear the Lord, and turn away from evil. It will be healing to your flesh and refreshment to your bones." (Proverbs 3:7-8)

"The fear of the Lord is hatred of evil" (Proverbs 8:13)

"The fear of the Lord prolongs life" (Proverbs 10:27)

"In the fear of the Lord one has strong confidence, and his children will have a refuge. The fear of the Lord is a fountain of life, that one may avoid the snares of death." (Proverbs 14:26-27)

"Better is a little with the fear of the Lord than great treasure and trouble with it." (Proverbs 15:16)

"The fear of the Lord is instruction in wisdom." (Proverbs 15:33)

"By loyalty and faithfulness iniquity is atoned for, and by the fear of the Lord a man avoids evil." (Proverbs 16:6)

Something's Missing - The Fear of the Lord

"The fear of the Lord leads to life; and he who has it rests satisfied; he will not be visited by harm." (Proverbs 19:23)

"The reward for humility and fear of the Lord is riches and honour and life." (Proverbs 22:4)

"Let not your heart envy sinners, but continue in the fear of the Lord all the day. Surely there is a future, and your hope will not be cut off." (Proverbs 23:17-18)

There is much spoken of today concerning prosperity for God's children. In many African countries unbalanced church teaching on prosperity, signs and wonders, healing and deliverance is becoming a curse upon the Church there, desperate for an escape from the gripping poverty and sickness which is all around. The above scriptures clearly teach us that our focus is to be on the Lord Himself, to hold Him in awe, to fear His holy name and to live lives that truly honour Him. As we do this, the Lord promises to meet us at our point of need – all the above blessings are for those whose focus and experience is to fear the Lord.

Holy Lives: Preparing for the Return of Jesus

The New Testament writers exhort us to be eagerly awaiting the return of Jesus:

"While you wait and earnestly long for – expecting and hastening – the coming of the day of God …" (2 Peter 3:12, Amplified Bible)

"Awaiting and looking for the blessed hope, even the glorious appearance of our great God and Saviour Christ Jesus, the Messiah the Anointed One." (Titus 2:13, Amplified Bible).

"So Christ, having been offered once to bear the sins of many, will appear a second time, not to deal with sin but to save those who are eagerly waiting for Him." (Hebrews9:28)

Paul concludes his first letter to the Corinthian church by using the Aramaic word 'Maranatha'. This is probably one of the earliest (and briefest!) prayers of the first Church, preserved in the spoken language of that time and place. 'Maranatha' literally means 'Our Lord, come!' The same word is found in the 'Didache', an ancient church book of teaching, most probably written in the first century.

John ends his wonderful heavenly revelation with:

"He who testifies to these things says, "Surely I am coming soon." Amen. Come, Lord Jesus!" (Revelation 22:12)

This response of eager anticipation and longing for the return of Jesus is for believers of all ages. However, for our generation, which is highly likely to see this incredible event take place, it is all the more poignant. The question is how many of us are ready for His return? A large section of the Church today doesn't appear to have a clue as to the urgency of the days that we are living in. In the affluent West, the prospect of Jesus returning soon can sometimes be more of an inconvenience in the hedonistic lives of many believers!

In Ephesians chapter 5, Paul, in speaking about the marriage relationship between husband and wife, compares this to the relationship between Jesus, the Bridegroom, and the Church, His Bride. Paul clearly states that the purpose of Jesus' sacrificial love for the Church was:
"That He might sanctify her, having cleansed her by the washing of water with the word, that He might present the church to himself in splendour, without spot or wrinkle or any such thing, that she might be holy and without blemish." (verses 26 and 27)
Undoubtedly Jesus is returning for a Church which has been prepared and is walking in holiness. This is made very clear by the writer to the Hebrews who states:
"Strive for peace with all men, and for the holiness without which no one will see the Lord." (Hebrews 12:14).

This preparation of holiness is clearly echoed throughout the pages of the New Testament. Peter states:
"Since all these things are thus to be dissolved (i.e. the heavens and the earth dissolved with fire), what sort of persons ought you to be in lives of holiness and godliness ... Therefore, beloved, since you wait for these, be zealous to be found by Him without spot or blemish, and at peace." (2 Peter 3:11 and 14)

Something's Missing - The Fear of the Lord

Paul states in his letter to the Romans:

"Besides this you know what hour it is, how it is full time now for you to wake from sleep. For salvation is nearer to us now than when we first believed; the night is far gone, the day is at hand. Let us then cast off the works of darkness and put on the armour of light." (Romans 13:11-12).

Again in his letter to Titus he writes:

"For the grace of God has appeared for the salvation of all men, training us to renounce irreligion and worldly passions, and to live sober, upright, and godly lives in this world, awaiting our blessed hope, the appearing of the glory of our great God and Saviour Jesus Christ." (Titus 2:11-13)

Anything less than a holy walk and a holy lifestyle will mean that we are unprepared as believers for the wonderful return of Jesus for His Bride. This is why the Holy Spirit is wanting to restore the fear of the Lord to the Church today. Just as with the example of Ananias and Sapphira in the book of Acts, so the Spirit of Holiness will do everything possible in these final days to draw the attention of believers around the world to the awesome holiness of our God, resulting in a new understanding of the fear of the Lord, a prime motivation in restoring to us the need for a holy lifestyle. Expect to see God breaking into the Church, your church, in awesome acts of mercy, but also in judgment, in these last days, and all the more as the return of Jesus draws even nearer. This will be part of His final preparation to receive a Bride without spot and blemish.

Paul exhorts the believers in his second letter to the Corinthian church:

Something's Missing - The Fear of the Lord

"Since we have these promises, beloved, let us cleanse ourselves from every defilement of body and spirit, and make holiness perfect in the fear of God."

There is no doubt that the fear of the Lord, which is birthed out of a fresh revelation of God's holiness, and an understanding of God's requirement in us for holy living, is key to preparing the Church, and each individual believer for the return of Jesus.

The book of Proverbs states:

"The fear of the Lord is hatred of evil" (Proverbs 8:13), meaning that to truly fear God will result in a hatred of anything that we know is offensive to God. Later in the same book, the writer declares:

"By the fear of the Lord a man avoids evil." (Proverbs 16:6). Again, a true fear of God will motivate us to turn away from all sin, thereby avoiding God's judgment upon our lives.

Let's seek God afresh for a new revelation of who He is, especially a revelation of His awesome holiness. Undoubtedly, this will result in us coming to a place where we truly understand what it is to fear the Lord, which will enable us to walk in holiness and righteousness before Him. Then we will cry out in eager and ready anticipation:

Maranatha!

Come, Lord Jesus!